GET CLEAR CAREER ASSESSMENT

FIND THE WORK YOU'RE WIRED TO DO

Whatever you do,
work at it with all your heart.
—Colossians 3:23 NIV

GET CLEAR CAREER ASSESSMENT

FIND THE WORK YOU'RE WIRED TO DO

BY KEN COLEMAN

Editor: Kris Bearss
Cover Design: Weylon Smith, Chris Carrico
Interior Design: PerfecType, Nashville, TN

ISBN: 979-8-887820-23-1

Printed in the United States of America

24 25 26 27 28 JST 5 4 3 2 1

CONTENTS

CONTENTS

INTRODUCTION
Imposter Syndrome

There's a phrase that gets thrown around the workplace a lot today: *imposter syndrome*. The phrase is used so often that many people will say they have imposter syndrome but not fully understand what that means.

Imposter syndrome is basically doubting your own skills and abilities to do the work you find yourself doing. Perhaps you're surrounded by people who come across as (or actually are) super professionals in what they're doing. Perhaps you feel some pressure because you don't have the same amount (or quality) of education as someone else. Imposter syndrome happens when you start comparing your work to someone else's and begin putting down your own work or seeing it negatively.

Some people have described imposter syndrome as overwhelming feelings of inadequacy that hang on even with the presence of success. Someone exhibiting imposter syndrome might feel that their work—say, as a designer—is not as good as other designers even though direct leaders praise and display the incredible work he or she is doing.

Psychology Today, in an online article about imposter syndrome, described it as people who "believe that they are undeserving of their achievements and the high esteem in which they are, in fact, generally held. They feel that they aren't as competent or intelligent as others might think—and that soon enough, people will discover the truth about them."[1]

An article in *the Harvard Business Review* identified some common thoughts and feelings of those who exhibit imposter syndrome:

> "I must not fail."
> "I feel like a fake."
> "It's all down to luck."
> "Success is no big deal."[2]

It's not uncommon to feel these types of feelings. In fact, many people experience them at some point in their work.

---

1. "Imposter Syndrome," psychologytoday.com (n.d.), https://www .psychologytoday.com/us/basics/imposter-syndrome#:~:text=People%20 who%20struggle%20with%20imposter,discover%20the%20truth%20 about%20them/.
2. Gill Corkindale, "Overcoming Imposter Syndrome," *Harvard Business Review* (May 7, 2008), https://hbr.org/2008/05/overcoming-imposter -syndrome/.

What I perceive from those who express feelings of imposter syndrome is just old-fashioned fear and doubt. The good news is, imposter syndrome is not a disease. This also means you're not a fraud; you're a genuine person doing your very best at the work assigned to you.

If you're experiencing doubt in your work right now, that tells me you're either trying to move forward or you want to move forward. Good! That's exactly what I want to address in this book.

So let's talk about what doubt really is. Doubt comes when you don't believe that something really good can happen to you or for you. Some of you who are picking up this book don't believe you can actually find the work you love that lights you up. You don't believe you can find the thing you love to do and actually get paid for it, let alone become prosperous as a result of that work.

A great way to overcome imposter syndrome, in my opinion, is to make sure you are operating in your strengths and passions. The *Get Clear Career Assessment* will identify your top talents, top passions, and top mission. You'll be able to use that information to find work that matters to you. When you're operating in your top talents and passions, you'll find there isn't a lot of room for imposter syndrome. It's much easier to be confident in what you're producing when you're doing what you do best and working on something you love doing.

I'm excited to walk you through this journey of personal discovery. This book, and the included assessment, will point you toward the work you were meant to do.

HOW TO USE THE
ASSESSMENT AND BOOK

You're about to discover how to find the work you're wired to do. That clarity will give you the confidence you need to move forward and make the contribution to this world that only you can make. And that's great because the world needs what you have to offer!

Here's how to use the *Get Clear Career Assessment* and this book.

Step 1: Tear out the Assessment code card from the back of this book.

Step 2: Follow the instructions on the code card to take the *Get Clear Career Assessment.*

Step 3: Review your PDF Assessment results (they'll come in an email).

Step 4: Read this book to better understand your results.

Step 5: Use the questions in this book to guide your next steps.

Remember: You were created to fill a unique role. You are needed. You must do it!

WORK DOESN'T
HAVE TO SUCK

I will never, ever forget that day for as long as I live.

It was a hot and steamy summer day on the coast of Virginia. I was a 19-year-old who had just recently started a summer job on a construction crew—a job my dad had landed for me. My job was to show up a lot earlier than everyone else so I could get everything ready for the crew.

I started by dead-lifting 50-pound bags of mortar, pouring the mortar into a giant mixer, adding water, and mixing it all up. Then I dumped the mortar into a wheelbarrow, pushed it around the jobsite obstacle course, and shoveled it out onto the various mortar boards, repeating the process until all the mortar boards were full.

Next, I grabbed the brick tongs—a crazy tool I'd never heard of before that made it possible for me to carry a dozen bricks at a time. I'd use the tongs to carry a set of bricks in each hand (two dozen bricks total, about 100 pounds) and stack them near all the mortar boards. That way the crew could hit the ground running when they arrived.

Basically, my job was to mix cement and carry bricks around the entire jobsite all day. All day . . . every day.

Here's what makes this story funny. At the time, I was only 130 pounds soaking wet. Skinny arms and skinny legs were not the best tools for hauling bricks all day. On this particular day, the temperature was already pushing 100 degrees with crazy-high humidity, providing a "feels like" temperature of something like 400 degrees! I was already suffering. And on this fateful day, it wasn't even lunchtime yet—it was only 11:00 a.m.

The exact time is burned into my memory. You'll understand why in a moment.

Let me describe the scene here. I was at my breaking point physically and mentally, and my 19-year-old self was done. I'd had enough. But my dad had gotten me the job, so quitting was not an option. But I needed to escape. So where do you escape to when you're on a construction site?

I began to scan the construction site for some place—any place—where I could go to be alone for a few minutes and take a break from it all. And then it appeared, almost like an oasis. Off to the side, on a bit of a grassy knoll, I saw it with the sun glimmering off the roof. It was a big, beautiful, orange . . . porta-potty!

You need to understand that I was so emotionally broken on this day that not only did I consider standing inside a large plastic sauna full of dirty, stinky excrement, but I did in fact make that move. I know, it sounds stupid to me too when I look back. I stepped inside, closed the door, and spun the handle to make sure everyone outside knew *this* booth of solitude was "occupied."

And let's be clear about this particular porta-potty. If you're rating bathrooms on a scale from the Ritz Carlton at the top to the Waffle House in Red Dirt, Mississippi, at the bottom . . . this porta-potty was from the seventh circle of hell. No joke. The only people using it were ones whose diet consisted of whatever was rotating on the hot rack at the gas station down the street. You know what I'm talking about.

You're probably thinking, *Seriously, Ken? You went and stood inside a porta-potty to escape the jobsite?* Yeah, I did. Why would I do that? It was because I was so miserable in that job. It was overwhelming. It was literally soul-sucking, and I hated every minute of it! I just had to escape.

Now I admit, that's an extreme story, not to mention gross (though I did learn the valuable lesson of mouth-breathing on that fateful day). But I share it because, in that moment of hot, disgusting clarity, I realized I didn't belong in that job. That's not what I was wired to do. I wasn't very good at it, I didn't enjoy it, and it wasn't going to be part of my future. I had no interest in construction—it was just a summer job and a paycheck. But it had turned into a nightmare situation for me. Thankfully, that experience woke me up to being intentional about doing work that I *did* enjoy.

You may not have stood in a hot and putrid porta-potty to consider your life's future, but you've probably had one or more dreadful jobs that made you wonder if there wasn't something else you could be doing. You may even be in a job like that right now—one that gives you a bad feeling every Sunday night when you realize you have to go back to work the next morning. You literally drag yourself out of bed on Monday just to get ready to go to work.

You're not alone in this.

Ninety thousand hours—90,000! That's the average amount of time Americans spend at work in their lifetime. It's a huge number, but think of *your* average workday. You probably spend more time working than doing any other activity in your life. Shouldn't you at least get some meaning out of that much time? That's not asking too much.

Here are some eye-opening stats from Gallup's 2023 report, "State of the Global Workplace":

- Less than a quarter (23 percent) of the world's workplace would say they're "engaged" at work.
- A majority (59 percent) of employees say they are "not engaged" at work.
- Almost one-fifth (18 percent) identify themselves as "actively disengaged" at work.
- Almost half (44 percent) of employees surveyed said they experienced a lot of stress the previous day.
- Over half (51 percent) of employees expressed some level of intent to leave their job.[3]

What stands out to me when I read this report is that nearly 80 percent of the people who work are just going through the motions with negative emotions. Their bodies are busy, but their souls left their bodies a long time ago. They're working—but not at their best. They're doing just enough to not get fired.

Nearly 80 percent of the people who work are just going through the motions with negative emotions.

Yikes! No wonder zombie movies and TV shows are so popular!

---

3. "The State of the Global Workplace: 2023 Report," Gallup, https://www.gallup.com/workplace/349484/state-of-the-global-workplace.aspx/.

Work can make us miserable, bore us to tears, or give us energy. We can leave work feeling completely fulfilled or completely drained. Or maybe you relate to my feelings of my soul being sucked out of me. When this happens, we naturally disengage. The stress from being in a place you don't want to be negatively affects your physical health, your sleep, and your relationships inside and outside the workplace.

The effect on your mental health is scary. It doesn't take many days of going through the motions with negative emotions to slip into discouragement, disengagement, and eventually depression. When your job doesn't matter to you, you soon begin to believe that you don't matter either. Life is too short to work in a place where you feel diminished and depleted.

I've been there. It's terrifying to feel like you have nothing special to offer. There's no bigger lie. Instead, here's the truth: you *do* matter because you *do* have something special to offer through your work. If you're searching and haven't found your niche yet, give yourself grace. You haven't wasted your life, and you're not a failure. You're here in this moment, reading this book, because you realize that receiving 26 paychecks in a year is not what you were born to do. Be grateful that it didn't take a moment of smelly reflection inside a steaming porta-potty to help you realize that.

The secret to winning in your work is to get in the right seat on the right bus. The *right seat* is where you're using what you do best to do work you love in order to produce results that matter deeply to you. The *right bus* is where you're recognized and rewarded for your unique contributions, and you have a relationship with your leader. That relationship is defined by the leader caring about you personally and developing you professionally.

Now is the time to choose to move from being exhausted *by* work to being energized *to* work.

If you're unhappy, uncertain, or unfulfilled in the work you're doing right now, this is the book and tool for you. The *Get Clear Career Assessment* will provide the awareness, confidence, and direction you need to pursue doing work that you were born to do. Let's go!

SECTION 1

AWARENESS

2

WIRED FOR WORK

This book and the *Get Clear Career Assessment* are designed to help you answer one of the most important questions you'll ever ask: "What should I do with my life?"

The *Get Clear Career Assessment* (one access code is included with this book) will walk you through your own discovery process, asking the key questions. All you have to do is answer honestly and instinctively. Re-read that sentence. It's very important that you don't overthink the questions and try to answer to make yourself look a certain way.

After you've completed the assessment questionnaire, you'll receive a PDF with your complete results. In those results you will find a ton of information based on your responses.

Let's also be clear that there isn't an assessment or a person out there who can tell *you* exactly what *you* need to be doing for work. There just isn't. But I can tell you that this book and assessment will give you the self-awareness you need to discover who you are, what you want to do, why you want to do it, where you can do it, and how you can get there. That's a big promise, but I assure you, that's where you're headed.

HOW THE ASSESSMENT WORKS

The *Get Clear Career Assessment* is a tool that helps you find the work you are wired to do. It gives you awareness of how you are uniquely designed by focusing on three specific "wires":

1. *Talents*—what you do best
2. *Passions*—the types of work you love doing
3. *Mission*—a result that you care deeply about

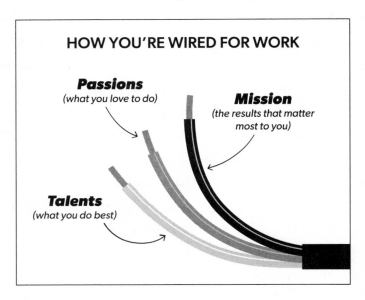

The assessment gives you a detailed report of what you do best (Talents), what you enjoy doing most (Passions), and the mark you most want to make (Mission). Then those results are summarized into a Purpose Statement that will give you clarity and confidence to move forward to do the work that you were born to do.

Before we get too far, I need to be clear about something. The *Get Clear Career Assessment* is *not* a personality test (like the Enneagram), and it's *not* a work communication tool (like DISC), and it's *not* a job predictor. The assessment will *not* show you exactly where you should be working. Only you can make that decision.

If you haven't yet taken the *Get Clear Career Assessment*, stop right now and do it. After completing the assessment, you'll receive your results. As a heads up, you're going to see a lot of details, which may feel overwhelming at first. But don't worry, I'll explain everything.

The focus of your results is the identification of each of your top talents, top passions, and your top mission. Be sure to read everything that's included with them and consult the explanations that have been provided. The rest of this book will help you get clarity from your results, and the next three chapters will further unpack your report. I want us to be on the same page so that you get the most out of the assessment.

Note: The glossary in the back of the book (starting on page 101) includes all the descriptive information for each of the 12 Talents, 15 Passions, and 6 Missions.

TALENTS

What you do best

3

UNDERSTANDING YOUR
RANGE OF TALENTS

While I was testing the content in the *Get Clear Career Assessment*, I sent a copy to my good friend Bill. I asked him to work through it and then give me some feedback. When we had a chance to talk about it, I asked, "So, what did you think of the assessment?"

Bill said, "Well, I've got 15 or 20 things I'd like to review with you."

He began rolling through his feedback. At one point he remarked, "I thought it hit me right on except for one of the Talent results. I think that one's off." I asked him which Talent descriptor he was referring to.

"The talent of Inspection," he replied.

As we talked, I realized he was getting hung up on the word *Inspection* and missing the assessment summary describing that particular talent. I asked Bill to read aloud the description that was included for Inspection. It begins:

> You're highly observant and you catch the details that other people miss. You have an ability to accurately critique the world around you. You process things efficiently while seeing a variety of perspectives and weighing all the possibilities effectively.

The idea is that people with this talent walk into a room and are able to immediately notice all the things that could be improved on.

Something clicked, and Bill started laughing.

"Do you remember how you started this call?" I asked. "You told me you had 15 or 20 things you wanted to get to."

"Oh, wow! I get it now!" he replied. A lightbulb had gone on for him when he realized this description was completely accurate.

That same thing has happened numerous times with people I've talked to after they've completed the assessment. So make sure to read through the description of each term in your assessment results; don't just judge your results by the label heading. The assessment may use a term differently than you're used to. What you're looking for is whether the *descriptive information* feels right in your gut.

TALENTS—WHAT YOU DO BEST

Quite simply, your talents are what you do best. A great visual is to think of your talents as power tools that allow you to do excellent work. Your *Get Clear Career Assessment* results will identify your top three talents.

Think of your talents as power tools that allow you to do excellent work.

I believe every skill can be put into one of 12 talent buckets. In your assessment report, the initial focus is on your top three talents. I like to refer to those as your super talents. It's important that you also review and understand the other nine talents—your solid talents and your subpar talents. Understanding your complete range of talents will lead to greater self-awareness that will allow you to be effective and excel in your work.

Your Super Talents

The first and most important talent category is your super talents. They are *super* because this is where you're at your best. When you're using your super talents, you stand out and give yourself the competitive edge to move up.

I want you to think of your super talents as your power tools. Sure, hand tools will get the job done, but not as effectively as a power tool. For example, let's say you have an old-school hand saw and a powered circular saw. They'll both cut wood, but the circular saw will do it faster, more accurately, and more efficiently.

Your super talents help you identify specific types of work that you would do well. My super talents are Communication, Persuasion, and Instruction. I use them when I'm engaging with people and sharing ideas. So anytime I'm interviewing a guest on my show, speaking on a stage, writing a book, or contributing on a news show, I'm working at my best because I'm using my best talents.

If you want to do great work, commit to learning how to improve your super talents and exercising those super talents. Do that and you will experience flashes of brilliance. Keep doing that and you will produce greatness. Find a job that allows you to spend most of your day using your super talents and you will not only deliver great results, but you'll feel great as you do it!

Your Solid Talents

These are things you're good at—not great at, but good. Your solid talents are important because they support and enhance your super talents. Because humans are wired for growth, we crave the challenge of getting better. Your solid talents give you an opportunity to grow and develop additional super talents.

Using myself as an example again, remember that my super talents are Communication, Persuasion, and Instruction. In my work, I spend the majority of my time in four roles: interviewing others, coaching individuals, giving commentary on my show and on television, and speaking to live audiences. There is excellent alignment between my super talents and my time.

My three solid talents are Discernment, Imagination, and Connection. How can I turn those solid talents into super talents? With Discernment, I need to learn more about body language and psychology and become a better listener. For Imagination, I need to carve out time for thinking, participate in collaborative brainstorms, and learn more about how the brain creates ideas. Finally, with Connection, I need to be intentional to spend time meeting acquaintances, showing up at gatherings, and seeking out people I want to learn from.

Consistent action toward these goals will, over time, allow me to grow my solid talents into super talents. Adding more super talents to your own tool belt increases your professional and financial growth. This also leads to more wins in the workplace.

Your Subpar Talents

Your subpar talents are the ones you suck at, or you're average at best. Don't worry—you didn't fail this part of the assessment. But let's go ahead and address the elephant in the room.

The idea of ignoring your weaknesses, which we are referring to as your subpar talents, is countercultural. Most of your life you've been told to work hard to make your weaknesses a strength. This is the silliest idea on the planet. Have you ever heard anybody say they wanted to take an "average" vacation, take their date to an "average" restaurant, or cheer for an "average" sports team? (Average sports teams just make their fans mad and get their coaches fired!) So why would you want to spend most of your time at work doing things you're just average at?

The reality is that average work and sucky work don't get promoted and don't get paid well. You can spend an inordinate amount of time trying to improve in these areas and you'll still be average. You're much better off spending any extra time you have working to improve your solid talents.

The reality is that average work and sucky work don't get promoted and don't get paid well.

When I was in middle school, my parents suggested that I learn to play an instrument and join the concert band. I decided on the trumpet, a decision I regret to this day! I tried. I really did. I practiced and practiced, but it didn't help. Honestly, I didn't like playing the trumpet, and I was just average (if that). Despite all my faithful and miserable practice, I never made it past third chair. I eventually quit because I had greater ambitions than being a third-chair trumpet player.

I want you to be aware of these subpar talents—and understand that someone else is super where you suck. This is great news because it means you don't have to waste your time constantly eating failure, trying to turn a subpar talent into a solid talent, let alone a super talent. That just leads to nothing but frustration. But the understanding your assessment results provide can free you to start focusing your energies in ways that will fulfill you and bring you success.

Talent Information

As you review your three top talents in your *Get Clear Career Assessment* results, you'll see four sections of information for each talent. The purpose of this information is to paint a general picture of you—a picture that will allow you to see yourself the way the world sees you. This is a general description of you, not a perfect, word-for-word analysis. Here's what you'll find:

- **Talent Summary**

  This paragraph provides a high-level description of what this talent looks like when it's used in the world of work. The description has multiple points of view to help you see yourself using this talent. This section also highlights the specific areas of work where this talent is most often used. This is a great place to explore which of these types of work might appeal to you.

- **How You Wow Others**

  These words and phrases are practical examples of how you use the talent to impact others—and do it with impressive results. This is not a complete list, so the way your talent gets expressed is not limited to what's here. But keep an eye out for some sort of connection point to your talent.

- **What Others Say About You**

  This is a list of compliments that people may give you. Whether or not these are the exact words, this list should spark your memory of the type of feedback you've received. This is an important exercise. It will remind you of where you shine!

UNDERSTANDING YOUR RANGE OF TALENTS

- **Talent Traps to Avoid**

  A talent is a strength—and every strength has its weaknesses. You can be highly talented in an area, but if you get out of balance, you can end up in a trap you created for yourself. Pay attention to these potential traps so you can set some personal boundaries in these areas.

Digging In:

What do you, and others, recognize to be your talents?

What types of tasks or assignments are easy for you?

Where have you experienced wins using your top talents?

PASSIONS

What you love to do

4

UNDERSTANDING YOUR
RANGE OF PASSIONS

A few years ago, I listened to a conversation between two cultural icons. Jerry Seinfeld was being interviewed by Howard Stern, and they were discussing what it takes to be great at what you do. Stern recalled his journey to radio and all the work it took to get him to where he was, and said, "It is possible to will yourself . . . to get what you want."

Seinfeld interjected, "What you were using, what Michael Jordan uses, and what I use, it's not will. It's love. When you love something, it's a bottomless pool of energy. . . . But you have to love it, sincerely. Not because you're going to make money from it or be famous or get whatever you want to get. When you do it because you love it, then you can find yourself moving up and getting really good at something."

That's a fantastic description of what I mean when I identify passion. Your passions are the things you love to do.

Seinfeld went on to say, "Will is like not eating dessert or something; it's just forcing yourself. You can't force yourself to do, to be, what you have made yourself into. You can love it. Love is endless. Will is finite. Real love is what enables you to accomplish anything. Not discipline, not work ethic. You gotta love it. If you love it, those other things come in behind it. They're the troops behind—love is the general."[4]

That's why working in your passions is so important. When you love what you do, it feels effortless. Your love—your passion—for what you do at work empowers you to do your work with excellence.

PASSIONS—WHAT YOU LOVE TO DO

When it comes to discovering how you're wired for work, your passions are the types of work you love to do. Think of a task or role that you look forward to in your job—something that

---

4. Howard Stern interview of Jerry Seinfeld, "Jerry Seinfeld on Whether '23 Hours to Kill' Is His Final Stand-Up Special and Which Other Comedian Could've Played Cosmo Kramer," *The Howard Stern Show*, Sirius XM (May 20, 2020), https://www.howardstern.com/show /2020/05/20/video-jerry-seinfeld-whether-23-hours-kill-his-final-stand -special-and-which-other-comedian-couldve-played-cosmo-kramer/.

causes you to lose track of time when you're doing it and, when you're done for the day, you can't wait to get back at it! As I like to say, this type of work gives you "the juice." Whichever tasks or roles have that effect on you, those are your passions.

In your *Get Clear Career Assessment* results, you'll want to focus on your top three passions, which I call your "I Love It" passions. It's important that you also review and understand the other 12 passions—your "I Like It" and your "I Could Do Without It" passions. But your top three passions represent the things you love doing the most. Those are the areas where you want to spend the majority of your time.

Understanding the full range of your passions will lead to greater self-awareness, which will give you more energy and enjoyment from your work. Listen, that's a huge deal. Energy and enjoyment are the types of things that keep people engaged in their work.

I Love It

Your top three passions represent work that you love to do. You get excited just thinking about it, and there's some real emotional attachment and energy behind it. When you're on the job, you're completely consumed by it. Time just seems to fly. Even when it's time to go home, you're excited to get back to it.

This work feels like it's a part of you because your heart is full anytime you do work you love. Remember, I call this feeling the juice! Your passions give you emotional energy that allows you to spend most of your day in a very positive mental and emotional state.

Looking at my own assessment results, my "I Love It" work is Leading, Performing, and Promoting. These top passions feel spot-on for me.

The basis of Leading is influencing others to act. One of the responsibilities of my job is to be an expert or thought leader. Communicating to lead others toward positive transformation makes my heart come alive. Even though I do this work in a very public role with a lot of pressure, the more pressure to perform, the more excited I get. Selling ideas and actions that aid and enhance transformation in people is one of my favorite things to do—that's Promoting. Many times, I do all three types of work at the same time. And I'll tell you, that's a really good day!

Ideally, you should spend about 75 percent of your day working within your top three passions. When that happens, your engagement, enthusiasm, and effectiveness will set you apart. Why? Because you're doing something you really love. And when you couple your top passions with your top talents—your excellence—that's when things really get done.

I Like It

In the same way that your solid talents support your super talents, your "I Like It" passions reinforce your "I Love It" passions. This type of work shines light on your path to your top passions. Think of your "I Like It" passions as stepping-stones to get you to the right spot. You want to get "I Like It" work on the path to "I Love It" work.

These passions do help to engage you on the job, but if you spend most of your time in "like," you'll eventually get bored—and that boredom can, over time, lead to burnout. So be prepared. Most people go through quite a bit of "I Like It" in order to get to "I Love It."

If you spend most of your time in "like,"
you'll eventually get bored—and that
boredom can, over time, lead to burnout.

My top three "I Like It" passions are Creating, Advising, and Advocating. I spent a lot of time doing work like this along the path to the work I'm doing now. Earlier, I shared that solid talents can be developed into super talents, and I believe that, over time, your "I Like It" work can transform into "I Love It" work. This happens when the application of the work changes. For example, I *like* brainstorming with others, but I *love* creating specific content that helps people see and reach their potential!

The potential danger with "I Like It" type of work is, you actually get *some* enjoyment out of it. But you're also probably going to be over it much faster. It's kind of like bubblegum—it's enjoyable for a few minutes but then you can't wait to spit it out.

"I Like It" work is best when it's surrounded by "I Love It" work. Ideally, spending about 20 percent of your day in this type of work is best. Keep in mind, this isn't a hard-and-fast percentage. There may be some weeks where you spend *all* your time in these types of tasks, but you certainly don't want to stay there indefinitely.

And don't get me wrong, you can absolutely win here with a nice salary and a nice career—but there will always be something missing because it's just "like." This can become a complacency trap, where you are comfortable in what you're doing while having this nagging feeling that there's more you could be doing.

I Could Do Without It

Let's admit it—there are some things you just don't like to do . . . and that's okay. The last section on your list of passions are things you don't enjoy or just downright hate. That doesn't make you lazy; it just means there's no positive, emotional connection at all for you in this type of work.

"I Could Do Without It" work is like going to the dentist or standing in line to renew your license plates. Nobody likes either of those. You only do it because you have to. That's what work in this area of your passions feels like.

A maximum of 5 percent of this type of work is the goal. Why? Because this type of work is at best super draining and, at worst, it's soul-sucking to the point that you may wander into a porta-potty for an escape.

So what do you do with these bottom-feeder passions? First, understand that there will be seasons where you'll do more of this work while paying your dues. Thankfully, this is temporary. Sometimes doing work you don't enjoy is just part of being an adult. I'm sure you've seen an "Adulting is hard!" meme. While that is true for some aspects of life, that shouldn't be the way you feel at work every single day. Just like you should do as little work as possible using your subpar talents, you want to do all you can to minimize and eliminate working within these no-passion areas.

Passion Information

As you review your top three passions, you'll see three sections of information for each passion. Remember, the purpose of this information is to paint a general picture for you—a picture that will allow you to see yourself the way the world sees you. It's not meant to be a perfect, word-for-word analysis of you. Here's what you'll find:

- **Passion Summary**

  This paragraph provides a high-level description of what this passion looks like when it's used in the world of work. The description has multiple points of view to help you see yourself engaging in this passion. You'll also be shown specific areas of work where this passion is most often recognized.

- **Work You Love to Do**

  These are practical examples of how this passion could be exhibited in your work. It's not an exhaustive list, and the way your passion may be expressed is not limited to what's here. But keep an eye out for the substance in each item and the connection point to a task or role that you love to do.

- **Passion Pitfalls to Avoid**
  Passion makes you run hot, and sometimes that can lead to burnout. When you love what you do and care deeply about it, there's always an opportunity for a misstep that leads to misunderstanding with the people around you. Awareness of these blind spots can help you avoid dangerous pitfalls.

Digging In:

When have you done something that really fired you up and lined up with your passions?

When you review your top three passions, what gives you the juice? What is it about them that helps excite you about work you really love to do?

MISSION

Results that matter to you

5

UNDERSTANDING YOUR
RANGE OF MISSION

I've got plenty of examples of how talents, passions, and mission work in real life, so allow me to share one example with you.

I work with a guy named Rick on the Ramsey team. He's a product writer, and his top missional result is Creation. He creates full-length outlines for books, projects, and curriculum. He's super detailed, enjoys digging into research, and is driven to provide the most accurate information he can. He loves what he does, and he's really, really good at it.

Rick's top mission (Creation), coupled with his passions (Analyzing, Researching, and Finishing), allows him to use his talents (Execution, Logic, and Organization) to do incredible work at Ramsey Solutions. He's a great example of someone who's using the things he does best to do work he really loves.

It's not uncommon to hear him tell a leader or other team member, "I love this!"—and it shows. And he's doing work that creates results that really matter to him.

The environment you grew up in, good or bad, often plays a huge role in shaping the type of results you want to produce. Rick's upbringing has really impacted his desire to see results from his work. Growing up, his dad told Rick two things related to work: "If a job's worth doing, it's worth doing right," and, "If you're going to do a job half-assed, don't do it at all." I love that. That's why Rick is so passionate about creating excellent work.

The truth is, all work creates results. But there's a huge difference between doing work that fulfills someone else's mission and doing work that produces the results *you* want to see. So when you find work that creates results that match up with your top mission, it's going to be a very rewarding field of work. Where you find work that engages your top passions and utilizes your top talents, that's where you're going to be the most successful, enjoy the most satisfaction, and find the greatest reward.

Your values are key. You'll be the most motivated to get out of bed, do an excellent job, deal with being passed over for a promotion, get past an idea being rejected, and continue to have staying power when your work lines up with your values.

This is huge for entrepreneurs. What will keep you going is that you care deeply about the results your business and your work are providing.

But where does that motivation come from? I want to give you a bit more background here. Going into the development of the *Get Clear Career Assessment*, I did a lot of research regarding motivation. There are two types of motivation: intrinsic—you do something because you *want* to do it; and extrinsic—you do something because you *have* to do it.

Only *you* can motivate you. Really. The idea that you can sit and listen to a motivational speaker for a couple of hours and be all set to go out and do something is just false. Sure, the speaker may inspire you, but that's different from true motivation. True motivation is when someone gets up at 5:00 a.m. to exercise because they enjoy the mental and physical benefits.

Extrinsic motivation is really manipulation. Let me illustrate this.

As a child, I was motivated to clean my room because my mom said if I didn't clean my room, I couldn't go out with my friends. Yes, she was teaching me responsibility, but I only did it because of the penalty or reward. That was purely extrinsic motivation. As a kid, I could care less whether my room was clean or not. I did it because I wanted to see my friends. I did it to avoid the punishment of not being with my friends.

True intrinsic (internal) motivation is when you do something because you really want to. Some people will say it's the mental shift of *I get to do* instead of *I have to do*. While that's good, it can feel a bit soft. When you think, *I WANT to do . . .* , that's coming from deep inside you. Now you are committed. This is a game changer.

It's what your mission is about—it's what truly drives you to do your work.

MISSION—RESULTS THAT MATTER TO YOU

The third section of your *Get Clear Career Assessment* identifies your top missional result. Like we just talked about, all work produces some sort of result. Your top mission describes the work result that matters most to you. It points to what you deeply care about contributing to the world through your work. This is your "why"—your motivation—at work.

The results of work can be grouped into six categories of mission. We'll dig into your top missional result, but it's also important to review and understand the other five missions.

Your top mission is referred to as "I Care Deeply," followed by the "I Connect with It" and "I Couldn't Care Less" mission results. Let's explore these three possible feelings about what your work produces. Understanding your range of mission will

44

lead to a greater self-awareness that will motivate you to do great work.

I Care Deeply

I want you to pay attention to the "I Care Deeply" work—this top missional result should be very personal to you! You see the results of your work as a crusade that must be waged and won. Your work provides a vital solution to a big problem that specific people have.

Every time I say, "You matter, you have what it takes, and the world needs what you have to offer," I'm talking about your mission combined with your top talents and top passions. Your mission is where your personal values become professional results. Your top mission helps you identify the type of result you want to make in the world through your work. You're never going to be truly fulfilled and you'll never operate at your best if you're not spending the majority of your time delivering this kind of result.

Your mission is where your personal values become professional results.

How can you know if what's listed as your top mission is truly what matters most to you? Good question. To help you with that, let me ask you a few questions:

- *Which results from your past have mattered so deeply that they still make you proud to this day?*
- *Where do you volunteer?*
- *What types of causes inspire you or deeply concern you?*
- *What have you done for the sake of others that you feel privileged to have been involved in?*

Take some time to answer each question. Your answers will begin to describe the type of results that matter most to you.

As you review your *Get Clear Career Assessment* results, does your top mission line up with your answers above? Knowing what you care deeply about equips you to look for work that helps you move toward those results using your top talents and top passions.

I Connect with It

For a number of people, their top two or three missional results could probably swap places easily. That's normal. Nothing to worry about! Generally, though, these results are important to you but they're not your top driver.

What you *will* find is that just as your solid talents support your super talents and your "I Like It" passions fuel your "I Love It" passions, your "I Connect with It" results operate hand-in-hand with your "I Care Deeply" work. Don't discount these—your "Connect" results are a part of who you are. Not only do they matter to you, but they help influence the type of work you'll do.

Your ideal work situation is one in which the results that you connect with happen naturally as you work to deliver the result you care deeply about. If you're working in your sweet spot, you'll see a clear tie between your "Connect" results and your "Care Deeply" result.

Looking again at Rick, who works on my team, his "I Connect with It" results are Achievement, Efficiency, and Influence. This means that while he's most driven to create content that changes lives, he wants to deliver his work with excellence and in a timely manner. This is exactly how your ideal work should look—a blending of your top missional results.

I Couldn't Care Less

The final two words on your Mission results page are identified as "I Couldn't Care Less." That may seem harsh. You might even look at each of those identifiers and think, *I sometimes care about that.* However, you're definitely not consistently fired up to deliver those results because they aren't your primary focus. They could be seen as just the basic requirement for you to keep getting a paycheck.

You don't want to be spending a lot of time on the job delivering these results. When the results of your work don't matter to you, you're on a slippery slope. Once you start thinking that your work doesn't matter, it can lead to thinking that *you* don't matter. And that's dangerous. As best you can, don't just limit your exposure to this type of work but avoid it. Long-term, it will just crush your soul.

Mission Information

As you review your top missional result, remember that this is general information designed to help you see a picture of results that move your heart. You may not resonate with every word, but you should see yourself in the description. For your top missional result, you'll find three sections of information:

- **Mission Summary**

  As with the talents and passions summaries, this paragraph provides a high-level description of what your mission looks and feels like. The paragraph should reveal what drives you and what leaves you with a feeling of significance. You want to validate if this information feels right in your gut. The general descriptions here should trigger a sense of what really matters to you.

- **Results That Fire You Up**

  This section offers a few practical examples of results that you want to make a reality. No one has to motivate you to achieve these results. While this is not an exhaustive list, some of the phrases should help you recognize and identify what you like to put into the world.

- **Mission Missteps**

  You care deeply about these results. Because your heart is involved, you might lose your head or operate with blinders on. This section points out areas where you can get in your own way or blind spots that will keep you from experiencing the results that matter the most to you. Keep these missteps at the top of your mind to avoid frustrating detours.

Digging In:

What parts of your work are creating results that matter to you?

What parts of your work are not creating results that matter to you?

What types of tasks or efforts give you energy? Which ones drain your energy?

6

DISCOVERING YOUR PURPOSE

Talents, passions, and mission. When they all come together, something fantastic happens. You end up doing work that truly matters to you—it's something you love, it's something you do well, and it produces the results you want to see. When someone is actually doing work that fulfills their purpose, it's a beautiful thing.

Rick Rubin is a legend and recognized as one of the most influential and sought-after music producers in history. He's well known for finding and developing new artists and launching incredible music careers. His own career began while he was a college student at New York University. The famous Def Jam Records was actually started in Rubin's dorm room—with the first hit being "I Need a Beat" by LL Cool J in 1984. That single quickly sold 100,000 copies!

If you haven't heard of Rubin, you've most likely heard music that he has produced, including songs from artists such as the Beastie Boys, Run-DMC, Public Enemy, Sir Mix-A-Lot, the Red Hot Chili Peppers, Mick Jagger, Neil Diamond, Adele, Tom Petty, and even Johnny Cash's comeback effort, American Recordings. Those are just a few of the more than 120 artists he's worked with since he started over 40 years ago.

In 2023, Rubin sat down for an interview with *60 Minutes.* When asked if he played any instruments, Rubin said, "Barely." He added that he doesn't know how to run a soundboard and basically has no technical ability. He also said, "I know nothing about music" (as in music theory). However, what Rubin does have is an incredible ear for music. He said, "I know what I like and what I don't like. And I'm decisive about what I like and don't like."

So what makes Rick Rubin *the* guy you need when you want to produce a hit song? He said it's "the confidence I have in my tastes and my ability to express what I feel that has proven helpful for artists." Rather than calling himself a music producer, he often refers to himself as a music "reducer" because he always wants to strip songs down to the essentials to get a true feel for where the music is leading him.[5] Rubin has

---

5. Anderson Cooper interview of Rick Rubin, "In Shangri-La with Music Producer Rick Rubin," *60 Minutes* (May 28, 2023), https://

explained, "What I do is give an artist the space to create. They tell me what they need to be successful."

Once, when asked if he always knew he would work in music, Rubin said, "I'll put it like this: The person that I am and the things that I like led me to music." In another interview, he said of the early years, "I always loved music. From the time I was a child, it was always the most important thing in my life." He also admitted, "I didn't know that I would have a job doing this. I did it because it was something I loved—and it turned into a job, which is unbelievable and I'm still shocked. I didn't know there was such a thing."[6]

Rubin has always liked being creative and helping artists do what they love. He found avenues to use his talents, passions, and mission to impact music. He does a wide variety of things that help other people create music. He knows who he is, what he likes, and it led him on a path.

At the end of the *60 Minutes* interview, Anderson Cooper pointed out that Rubin doesn't want people to hear an album and say, "That's a Rick Rubin album." No," the famous

---

www.cbsnews.com/news/rick-rubin-60-minutes-transcript-2023 -05-28/.
6. Krishnan Guru-Murthy interview of Rick Rubin, "Rick Rubin: The Legendary Music Producer on Working with Run DMC, Slayer and Johnny Cash," Channel 4 News (January 14, 2023), https://www .youtube.com/watch?v=WudmmlYnx8c/.

producer replied. "I want them to say, 'This is the best thing I've ever heard,' and not know why."[7]

"I didn't know that I would have a job doing this. I did it because it was something I loved— and it turned into a job, which is unbelievable and I'm still shocked." –Rick Rubin

---

What drives Rick Rubin is producing music that moves people and makes them feel something. He has a talent for hearing good music and launching successful careers, he has a passion for music, and he wants music to move people.

Finding Your Purpose

Rick Rubin's story always motivates me because he's a fantastic example of someone doing what he does best, working at something he loves, and producing the types of results that really matter to him. And that can happen for you too.

After identifying your top talents, passions, and mission, your *Get Clear Career Assessment* results also give you a unique Purpose Statement. As a coach, this is my favorite part of the

---

7. Rubin, "In Shangri-La."

assessment! It's a reflection of the distinct way you're wired for work. Think of it as a high-level job description that's unique to you. When your talents, passions, and mission come together, you'll experience incredible clarity, confidence, and courage, allowing you to step out and pursue your purpose.

So how exactly do talents, passions, and mission relate to your Purpose Statement? Great question. Here's a way to think about this:

Talent is a *technical measure.*
Talent is what you're good at—you're just born with it. Talent is "how" you do things. Talent is always a clue to your passion and your mission.

Passion is an *emotional measure.*
Passion is what you love to do. It can be described as your "where"—as in, where you find energy and what lanes best use your top talents. Your passion is what makes you tick.

Mission is a *foundational measure.*
Mission is the "why" part of the equation, when you identify what results matter most to you. It's not just a "should be" or "could be"—it's a "must be" result for you. Your mission really is what gives you grit.

In my mind, the way this all comes together is not unlike a literal electrical wire. Granted, like most analogies, don't take this one too far or too literally. In electrical wiring, the "hot" wire is usually black or red. That's where the power comes from. Without the power, nothing's going to happen. The "neutral" or return wire is usually white. From an electrical standpoint, this wire is a current-carrying conductor that sends the current back to the power source. Basically, it keeps the power circulating and allows the "hot" wire to do its thing effectively. The "ground" wire is usually green or just bare copper. The ground is super important because it helps drive the electrical results in a safe way. You could say that the ground wire allows the electricity to produce the results that matter and in a way that matters. All three wires are needed for the safe and effective use of electricity.

So for our purposes related to how you're wired for work, let's identify that "hot" wire as your talents. These are the things that you're great at doing and where your working power is best displayed. The "neutral" wire is your passions. It's your emotional connection (what you love to do) that powers you to use your talents most effectively. Then you add in your "ground" wire with your mission—these are the results that matter most to you. Your mission is that foundational element that ties everything together; it grounds you and provides your why.

Just as all three wires are needed for the effective use of electricity, your work will be most successful and effective when you combine your talents, your passions, and your mission to achieve the results that matter most to you.

While you review your Purpose Statement, I want you to consider the following:

Working in Your Talents

When you're working only in your talents, you can be successful. Why? Because you're doing the types of things you do best. So, naturally, you're going to be successful using those talents. If all you're interested in is success, make sure your work is making the best use of your top talents.

Working in Your Talents and Passions

But if you couple your talents and passions—doing what you do best while doing what you love—you can experience success as well as find satisfaction in your work. That's easy to see because you end up doing what you love and using your top talents to do it. If job satisfaction is your desire, you need to find work that lets you use your talents doing something you love to do.

Working in Your Talents, Passions, and Mission

However, if finding significance—true significance—in your work and in your life is important to you, then you need to find work that combines your talents, passions, and mission. In other words, you're using what you do best to do work you love so that you produce the results that matter deeply to you. This is going to lead you to achieve success and experience satisfaction as well as discover significance in both your work and your life.

When you bring all of that together, your work will have purpose and produce results—results that matter to you. That's truly work that matters.

7

WHERE YOU ARE RIGHT NOW

When I coach people through the topics within their *Get Clear Career Assessment* results, my goal is to use their results to bring clarity to three points:

1. Who I am
2. Where I am
3. Where I want to go

Let's take some time to walk through these three points because I want you to have that same clarity related to your results. The assessment has provided you with a list of your top talents, your top passions, and your top mission. Your Purpose Statement puts all of that together. That is the first point. The assessment has shown you who you are.

You now have complete awareness of how you're wired for work. The next step is to match your talents and passions with the right seat on the right bus so you can see the results that matter most to you. It starts with honestly addressing the second point: where you are. Resolving that point will get you moving in the right direction to find the type of work you're wired to do. That's ultimately where you want to go, right?

Where you want to go is forward thinking. Before you can think forward, you need to identify where you are right now. Now that you have full awareness of your range of talents, passions, and mission, you'll want to work through a simple three-step process with that information. This process will help you evaluate where you are right now. The three steps are *accept*, *assess*, and *share*.

Accept Who You Are

You've already explored your *Get Clear Career Assessment* results to discover your top talents, passions, and mission. These represent what you do best, what you love to do, and the result that matters most to you. The listing of your talents and passions isn't just an arbitrary ranking. The assessment took all the responses you gave and presented a clear picture of who you are and how you're wired for work.

At this point, you want to strive to mentally accept the information you've been given about your talents, passions, and mission. You're accepting who you really are—not what a coach, teacher, or parent wanted you to be.

With this information, you can see where your desires and frustrations come from. There are things you desire in your work because that's how you're wired—you're passionate about it and those things motivate you. The frustrations you experience in your work typically come from doing things you don't do well and have no passion for—you're not experiencing the opportunity to work in your talents and passions.

It's important to accept how you're wired for work so that you're thinking and acting on purpose and with intentionality. Rather than doing something just because others say you're really good at it, you should be looking for work that you love to do. Your Purpose Statement points you in the right direction. And accepting how you're wired leads to full clarity—which is a great thing. You can now say, "This is who I am; this is how I'm wired. This is the real, authentic me."

Rather than doing something just because others say you're really good at it, you should be looking for work that you love to do.

When it comes to how you're wired, there's a big difference between knowing and believing. You can know in your head all the things you read in your assessment results, but you need to believe in your heart that this is what you're meant to do. Let me give you an illustration from my childhood.

When I was seven, my parents took me to the municipal pool and signed me up for swimming lessons. During those several weeks, I had no problem doing everything that was expected of me—I was able to swim in the pool easily. At the end of the course is when I faced my greatest challenge. Every kid was required to jump from the high dive and swim to the side of the pool in order to graduate from this particular course.

Just to be clear, this was a long time ago. The location of this dive, this death drop, was at the top of a 12-foot-high diving platform—a large, concrete structure with a metal ladder on the back. I climbed to the top of the tower with the other kids, no problem. I was near the back of the line as we inched up, one by one, toward the edge of the platform. No problem. I watched the kids in front of me each take their turn jumping off the tower, splashing into the pool, going under the water, and then swimming to the side of the pool. No problem, right?

Wrong! When I got to the front of the platform, I looked down. Granted, it was only 12 feet high, but it looked to me at age seven like I was diving into the abyss.

Everything about this was scary. My mom and dad were near the edge of the pool encouraging me to jump—but I just couldn't do it. I was scared to death and overcome with fear. I turned around and made the humiliating walk of shame back to the ladder and back down the tower. I failed the course.

The next year, my parents signed me up for swim lessons again. However, this year, as I stood on the edge of the platform, I jumped into the pool and swam to the edge—and graduated! What was the difference? I went from knowing to believing.

Here's what I mean. I knew I wasn't going to die because I had seen everyone else jump in, go under water, and swim to the side of the pool. Not one of them died. My mom and dad were cheering me on again too. They had faith in me. As I stood on the edge of the tower, I had a moment of clarity that gave me the confidence and courage I needed. I believed in my heart, not just in my head, that I could do it. I didn't just *know* it, I *believed* it. I actually believed I could jump off the tower, go deep under the water, pop back up, take a deep breath, and then swim to the side of the pool—and I did it.

When you look at your assessment results, you may *know* in your head that those things resonate with you and describe you. But you have to *believe*, and accept, that they are true of you. When you go from knowing to believing, you gain clarity. In my life, I've discovered that clarity leads to confidence, and confidence leads to courage. Accepting means that you absolutely believe your results because the evidence is in front of you. You make the choice to believe. And again, when you're clear, you become confident.

Have you ever driven in rain that was so hard or fog so thick you couldn't see, and all you could do was slow down or pull over to the side of the road? In that type of situation, you're paralyzed because the road can't be seen clearly. That paralysis keeps you from moving forward. But after the rain lets up or the fog lifts, and you can see again, you have the confidence you need to move forward.

So, when you're stepping out in confidence but run into an issue or something that slows you down (you lack the courage to keep going), you can retreat to clarity: *This is what I know about how I'm wired for work because of what I see in my assessment results and my Purpose Statement.* Once you re-establish that point of clarity, you'll be able to confidently and courageously move forward again.

Now you have a formula. Every time your confidence takes a hit, you can retreat to clarity.

Accept, the first step in this process, is all about your mindset. You need to believe that the things describing you are true. Acceptance gives you the right mindset to step out and make a change in what you're doing.

Assess Where You Are

Now that you know who you are, it's time to look at where you are right now. This is all about assessment and evaluation. What changes do you need to make?

Let's be honest, if you're reading this book and taking the *Get Clear Career Assessment,* you're probably looking for a change in your current reality. It may be a sense that something needs to be different or an inner drive to do something different. Either way, that's great. We can begin to work through it by first looking at where you currently are in your job.

What's your current seat on the bus? What does a typical day at work look like for you? Create a list of all the different things you do on a daily basis. Display a copy of your Purpose Statement from the assessment on your desk. For at least a week, take note of your daily tasks and your time.

Of all those everyday tasks, how many of them involve using your super talents? How much of your time do you spend on tasks that you love to do? How much of your time is spent producing results that really matter to you? Keep track of everything and give it an honest evaluation. It might even help you, especially if you're a visual learner, to chart out your time and list the tasks you're involved in.

For every task, ask yourself, *Does this boost me or drain me?* I suggest creating a page with two columns, one labeled *Boost* and one labeled *Drain*. Then list your various tasks in each column. It's a quick way to see where most of your work falls right now.

For every task, you need to ask yourself,
Does this boost me or drain me?

Charting out your time and energies like this will clearly show you where you're being drained. Often when people are feeling drained, they're spending too much time using their subpar talents and doing things they have no passion to do.

Next, compare your task chart to your Purpose Statement. How much of your time are you spending doing purposeful work based on your assessment? Ideally, as we've established, you want to be spending roughly 75 percent of your time using your top talents and top passions. You want your time to be spent doing the things that boost you.

This assessing process allows you to see where things may be off and where there's room for improvement. Many of you reading this book are probably realizing, *Hey, I need to make some changes!* Again, this is a mental shift that becomes a moment of clarity.

Here's an example of how this clicked with Rick on our publishing team. He had been at Ramsey Solutions for a couple of years and enjoyed most of his work. I say *most* because, while he was well respected by those he worked with, there was one aspect of his job that just seemed to drain him: the outlining of content for various books and projects. He found himself doing a lot of outlining, and he was starting to feel very depleted. The thing is, those of us who are his colleagues thought he was great at outlining content.

Rick discussed his feelings and frustrations with his leader, Allen. Allen asked Rick what types of things he felt he was good at. Rick said he enjoyed teaching and helping make complex ideas understandable and actionable. As they began to unpack the work of outlining, it became clear to Allen that this aspect of Rick's job was something that fit very well within his range of top talents and passions—he was just looking at it the wrong way.

Through their discussions and assessing of the situation, a lightbulb went off for Rick. He recognized that the outline work he was doing *was* essentially boiling down huge chunks of content into a manageable, easy-to-understand format. Once that mental shift took place, and Rick understood how who he is and what he does all fit together, he really took off in his work.

Once you've worked through the accept and assess steps, you're at a place where you recognize some practical and tactical changes that need to happen. That's clarity! Remember what you're shooting for. You want to make changes that will let you spend most of your workday using your super talents and spend the least amount of time possible using your subpar talents. You're looking for ways to delegate or eliminate work that involves using your subpar talents. This leads right into the third step . . .

Share Where You Want to Go

Sharing is all about communication—specifically with your leader. You'll want to share all the information you've learned about yourself and how you're wired to work. Your goal is to get yourself in the right seat on the bus, ideally at the company you're already at.

Most of the data I read reveals that most people don't really "hate" their jobs; they're just not engaged—and they hate not being engaged. Honestly, most people hate the thought of all that goes into having to change jobs: quitting, the job search, interviews, and the transition. Let me point out that the default response after getting your assessment results should not be, "Well, I need to leave my current bus to find another bus." You might need to make a change, but let's see if we can at least adjust what you're doing to get you into the right seat on the bus where you already work.

Before you begin looking to change jobs, set up a meeting with your leader. You have nothing to lose because you're now equipped with the information from the assessment. You have clarity on what you do best, what you love to do, and the result that matters most to you. You know who you are and what you want to do. And you know how much of that type of work you're actually doing today. Now, this is all about moving forward.

The first part of this specific step is to share what you're discovering with your leader. You'll quickly find out if he or she is open to working with you. Ideally, you want to be able to sit down with your leader, share your assessment results, and have a conversation that goes something like this:

> I've gone through this exercise and discovered a lot about myself and my work. There were many things I didn't realize about myself. And, honestly, this has been a bit of a lightbulb moment for me. Let me share my Purpose Statement with you.
>
> I've also evaluated what I do each day and identified the tasks that boost me and the tasks that drain me. I realize I'm going to be a lot more productive,

happier, and more engaged if I'm doing the types of things I'm best at and that I love doing. If I can move into these types of tasks, my engagement will go up, which means my productivity will go up.

I don't think I'm in the right seat right now, and I'd like to work with you on changing my seat. I believe that will make me even more productive. What do you think about this? Can we work together to make this happen?

This is a solution-based approach. You're talking with your leader and actually offering solutions to the situation. When you have your assessment results and your Purpose Statement, it's easy to show your leader what you do best, what you love to do the most, and what really matters to you. You'll be able to clearly discuss the types of tasks that could be tweaked, moved, or delegated, as well as the additional tasks you could pick up that would more closely match your talents and passions. The solution could be as simple as shuffling some tasks around within the team. This might even help the entire team be even more engaged and productive too!

Share with your leader all the tasks that boost you and all the tasks that drain you. (The hope is that you have a healthy leader who will work with you.) A healthy leader will say something like, "Alright, this is good information. Let's see what we can do to make this work out." If your leader and your co-workers are really plugged in, they'll be able to see the things that frustrate you in your work and the tasks where you excel. Your co-workers may say, "Yes, I know this frustrates you. I can help you with that if you would do this thing I don't enjoy but that I know you like to do." That's a great way to move in the right direction.

One of the leaders at Ramsey did this with his team. He had his entire team take the *Get Clear Career Assessment* and then he reviewed all their results. He began shifting work assignments, recognizing areas and tasks where team members excelled. He would point out which individuals were especially strong in particular areas and direct others who were struggling in those same areas to ask for help. Those little changes made the entire team stronger, more efficient, and more productive.

All the changes won't happen overnight—it will be a process. That's fine, as long as you're moving closer to doing the type of work that fits your talents and passions. The reason you want to share your assessment results with your leader and co-workers is for the goal of moving you into the right seat on the bus you're already on. Making these changes will make a massive difference in your work life!

I understand that every workplace is different. You may not have a regular pattern of one-on-ones with your leader. You may not even have an annual check-in with your leader.

Okay, then, set one up. Ask him or her for a meeting where you can discuss your role and your work responsibilities. If nothing happens after you've shared your results, or if your leader is completely unopen to discussing any changes, then you have your answer—this is not the right bus. That means you need to start looking for the right bus. But, if you share this information and your leader begins to make the moves and you see positive change, you just saved yourself a lot of frustration. Either way, you're no longer in a mindset of feeling stuck. And it's because you know who you are and what you want to do.

The second part of this step is to share your assessment results—along with what you discovered through the accept and assess steps—with your friends and acquaintances outside of work. Explain the type of role you really see yourself in. Now you have a narrative. When someone asks what type of work you want to do, you don't have to say, "I don't really know." Now you do know—you really know. You'll be able to say, "I want to use these talents to do this type of work that I really love because I want to see these types of results." Do you see how much more powerful and clear that is?

This is where opportunities will present themselves. Someone may respond, "My brother-in-law is hiring and looking for someone to do this type of work. You should go talk with him." And when you're looking for other jobs and interviewing, you can confidently share the type of work you're looking for because you've taken the time to accept and assess your results, and you have your Purpose Statement in hand. I'm telling you, this is a game changer.

ACTION

8

FOUR AREAS OF WORK

As I've looked over the world of work, figuring out the kind of work you were created to do is as simple as understanding the four basic areas of work: People work, Ideas work, Process work, and Object work. I believe all types of work can be put into at least one of these areas. For each area of work, ask yourself two questions:

1. *Am I good in this area of work?*
2. *Do I enjoy this area of work?*

Within these four areas, the *Get Clear Career Assessment* will show you how different applications of your talents and passions might be recognized. There are generally one or two areas of work where you'll naturally excel. And that's the type of knowledge that helps lead you toward clarity as well as success and satisfaction in the work you do. Having knowledge of where you excel points you in the right direction to find work in which you will excel.

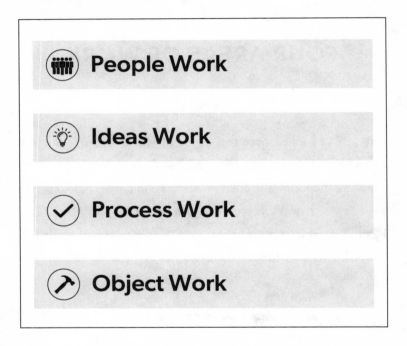

Your Purpose Statement is going to help you recognize if you would prefer People work, Ideas work, Process work, and Object work. Let me explain and then share an example with you.

People Work

If you're good at working with people and you love working with people, then you'll be most satisfied doing this
type of work. A good clue here would be to ask yourself,
*Does working with people give me energy or does it drain
me?* Those who prefer People work tend to be compassionate and empathetic. They enjoy focusing on people
problems. They feel fulfilled in advising, serving, and
encouraging others.

Ideas Work

If you're really good at working with ideas and love working with ideas, then you need to be doing work that is more
creative in nature. Again, start by asking yourself if this type
of work gives you energy or drains you. People who enjoy
Ideas work are often creative, imaginative, and insightful.
This type of work involves thinking and collaboration.

Process Work

Do you enjoy working with processes? Would you say you
love working with processes? If so, then finding work that
involves organizations and systems is where you need to look.
Process work includes checking boxes, efficiencies, solving
problems, bringing order to chaos, and providing excellence.

Object Work

If you're good at working with objects and you love working with them, you need to be doing some type of work that involves your head and/or your hands. Do you find joy in building or fixing? That's a good clue. Working with objects often involves working with your hands but can also include inventing or developing new things.

Identifying Your Primary Areas of Work

When you overlay your Purpose Statement with the area of work that best describes you, something wonderful can happen. You really begin to identify which kind of work is ideal for you. Let me give you a real-life example of how some of this plays out.

A guy called my show who wanted to be in some sort of creative role. He described himself as very creative, but he was working in a finance position. He said he was good with numbers and didn't hate working with numbers, but he *loved* the idea of doing something that was more creatively oriented. In other words, he was very good at Process work, and evidently a natural at it. He was a guy who's good with numbers, accounting, spreadsheets, and finances.

But, while he was good at Process work, he didn't love it. What he did love is creating things—and that's Object work.

He said he's a sculptor and enjoys it because he's working with his hands—taking ideas and creating something tangible. Since Object work is the kind of work he loves doing, he really needs to be in a job where he is working with his hands and creating things.

I've found it worthwhile to chart your assessment results using your top three talents and top three passions. This lets you visualize your results laid over the grid of the areas of work (from the Glossary section for each Talent and Passion). This is a huge help in your clarification process. Creating your own simple chart will help you plot where each of your top talents and top passions intersect with specific areas of work.

Going back to my team member, Rick—who works in publishing creating outlines and content for use in books and curriculum—this is what his chart looks like:

Areas of Work	People	Ideas	Processes	Objects
Talents				
Logic		X	X	
Execution			X	X
Organization		X	X	
Passions				
Analyzing			X	X
Researching		X	X	
Finishing			X	X
TOTALS	**0**	**3**	**6**	**3**

Rick is heavily weighted when it comes to Process work. Knowing the type of work he does, I can tell you this is absolutely correct. While Rick doesn't mind working with people and even leading people, he gets "the juice" when he's working within processes (creating outlines) and working through idea-based projects.

There's an extra layer of clarity when we add the next three highest-ranked talents and passions from his assessment to the totals above:

Areas of Work	People	Ideas	Processes	Objects
Talents				
Inspection		X	X	
Imagination		X	X	X
Justice	X	X		
Passions				
Creating		X		X
Making		X		X
Teaching	X	X	X	
TOTALS	**2**	**9**	**9**	**6**

As you can see, Rick's results are still heavily weighted in the Ideas and Processes spaces. This is an easy way to get a high-level view of which areas of work may be the best fit for you. This type of clarification can provide the inspiration you need to begin to explore a variety of work environments that maybe you haven't considered before.

This is a fun exercise that provides more direction as you begin to think about the type of work in which you would be the most successful and find the most satisfaction. A chart like this allows you to see which spaces, or areas of work, you should be in to be the most effective. Why? Because it measures what you're good at and what you enjoy doing. Maybe it will give you that little extra bit of information that causes a lightbulb to go off in your head and gets you going in the right direction.

I also want to say, don't get bogged down in where all your checkmarks land on the chart. What you're primarily looking for is a pattern. Pay attention to where the majority of your checkmarks are landing. This is simply a tool to guide you in further exploration.

Digging In:

In what two areas of work do most of your talents and passions fall?

In your work, how have you seen alignment with your talents and passions lead to wins?

9

RESULTS-FUELED
EXPLORATION

Now that you have your assessment results and have arrived at this point in the book, it's time to move on to your next steps. Practically speaking, you're ready to start looking—and find—the work you were born to do. You've identified who you are and where you are. Now you can turn your focus to identifying where you want to be. You're going to explore a variety of work options and then start selecting which one is the best fit based on your Purpose Statement.

At this point, when I'm coaching someone, I'll ask a series of three questions. I might vary the order of the questions depending on which area of work they score highest in, but I eventually get them to answer each of these questions:

- *Who are the people you most want to help?*

- *What problem or desire do you want to solve?*
- *What solution do you want to provide?*

These questions aren't necessarily sequential. For example, if someone scores highly on the People area of work, I'll lead with the people question. However, if someone scores highly in the Ideas or Processes area of work, I'll lead by asking them the question about what kinds of solutions they want to provide and then come back to the people question. Each of the three questions is important because they turn the dial in a specific direction that can be explored.

> ## *Who are the people you most want to help?*
>
> ## *What problem or desire do you want to solve?*
>
> ## *What solution do you want to provide?*

If you're people-oriented, start with that first question. If you're oriented toward ideas, processes, or objects, start with the second question and *then* answer the first one.

The reason this exercise is effective is because it will move you toward your heart—what moves and motivates you. I've used these three questions to help many people open their minds to new possibilities. These questions work because, ultimately, all areas of work lead to helping people in some way.

Digging In:

Answer these questions and then create a list of as many different work options as you can think of. You'll come back to this list in a bit.

Who are the people you most want to help?

What problem or desire do you want to solve?

What solution do you want to provide?

Exploring Your Options

Let me share an example that's in my book *From Paycheck to Purpose*, because it sheds some light on what you can do with your assessment results. This can help you take your results and turn them into something that will provide direction in finding work that you love to do and that matters to you.

Not too long ago I talked with a high school student, Caitlyn, who wanted to be a nurse—she just wasn't sure what type of nurse. After all, just like doctors, nurses can specialize in any number of fields: some work the admitting room or the emergency room; others love the operating room or physical rehab; and still others serve in geriatrics, intensive care, or the delivery room. And of course, there are dozens of places where a nursing degree can be put to use beyond a hospital, including retirement centers, schools, or addiction recovery facilities.

So I encouraged Caitlyn to make a list of different kinds of nurses such as trauma nurse, emergency room nurse, pediatric nurse, primary care clinic nurse, pre-op nurse (focusing on the clerical side of things), post-op nurse, and so on. Then, once she had a list of the different possibilities, I suggested she go back through her list and circle the options that stood out as something she was highly interested in and cross off the ones that she had no interest in. From her narrowed-down list, she had possibilities she could begin to explore. I told her if she had the opportunity to explore those different nursing jobs through an internship or shadowing situation, that would be even better.

Let's say she discovers that she's not cut out to be an emergency room nurse. That's okay; that's not a failure—that's clarity working for her! It's not a no, and she's not confused. She's one step closer to her yes. Medical doctors explore various areas of medicine during their rotations to find out which fits them best. Why not the rest of us?

Some preliminary online research would help Caitlyn determine any specialties or education she might need and what general qualifications she would need to move forward. As Caitlyn reviews the results of her assessment and begins to create a list of different nursing options, she's going to decide that most of those seeming "matches" are only a partial fit, and she'll eliminate them from her search.

While Caitlyn didn't have the benefit of the *Get Clear Career Assessment* to guide her toward work that aligned with her talents, passions, and mission, you do. Ideally, you want to find work that you're great at and you love doing. It really is an exploration process. But, rather than just a shot in the dark, the assessment identifies your top talents, top passions, and the result that matters most to you.

So, with your actual assessment results in hand, I want to encourage you to follow three simple steps: Clarify, Verify, and Explore. I spent a lot of time unpacking the entire process to clarify and verify in my book *From Paycheck to Purpose,* so I won't revisit all of that here. But I do want to provide some direction to help you in this process because these are important steps in doing work that matters to you.

First Step: Clarify

First, you need to clarify your results. This simply involves reviewing your assessment results. You want to check your initial gut reaction to what the assessment revealed as your top talents, top passions, and your main mission. Do the descriptions resonate with you? You should also ask friends who know you well to review your results. Are they mostly agreeing with your results and telling you this is on track; you're in the ballpark?

But don't stop there. Remember, as I explained earlier, some of the words I chose to use—to avoid overlap—may mean one thing in your mind but may be different from how I'm describing a particular talent, passion, or mission. So take some time to read the complete descriptions of each of your top talents, top passions, and top mission.

For every Talent description, you'll also see a list of some ways you might wow people with that talent as well as what others say about someone with that talent. Do those things describe you? Have you experienced anyone saying anything like that about you? That's the process of clarifying your results.

When you get to your Passion descriptions, you'll see some examples of tasks that relate to that passion. Again, as you clarify your results, do those tasks fit with what you love to do? And finally, when you get to your top Mission description, does the list of results that fire you up sound like you? Do you really get fired up by those results?

Clarifying your results is like following a trail of clues. As you examine your results, what patterns do you see emerging? Do those patterns accurately describe you? As you look at the descriptions, which key words make your heart jump a little? All of these little clues are like footprints leading in the direction of your Purpose Statement.

Clarifying your results is like following a trail of clues.

Create a list of various work opportunities that would allow you to use your talents and passions to do something that really matters to you. In Caitlyn's example, she identified a wide variety of nursing positions that could be a possible fit for her. At this point, you're not trying to pinpoint the "perfect" job—you're just trying to create a large list of opportunities that you could begin to explore.

Second Step: Verify

Now that you have your list of work opportunities, it's time to verify your results. Review your list and cross out any jobs that are a clear no for you. As you're exploring potential matches, don't worry if you seem to be saying, "No. Next!" a lot. Whatever you eliminate and whatever you keep in at this stage, your research has done its work. It's leading to clarity.

Another aspect of verifying is to get feedback from other people. Share your assessment results with others. Ask for feedback as to whether they see these things in you or if these things provide a good description of you. This will help ensure that you haven't overlooked something about yourself that others recognize. You don't want to operate in a vacuum as you're working through your assessment results.

Beyond verifying the assessment results, share the potential work opportunities you've listed with people who know you and ask if they could see you doing that type of work—and why.

Third Step: Explore

After you've taken some time to work through clarification and verification, it's time to engage in exploration. This process involves research, so you're going to need to set aside some time for gathering information. Dive in online and get any facts you can find for your potential work opportunities, including salary ranges and job availability.

Next, talk to some experts—the people doing the jobs you're interested in—to search beneath the surface and learn what's really involved in each type of work. Face-to-face, in-person conversations are the best way to do this, but video conferencing is another way to connect.

As you go through this process of exploration, you're essentially doing a term paper on every profession that intrigues you. You want to ask questions such as: What was each person's career path? Their background? How did they get hired? What programs or training did they need? Also, what is their day-to-day experience: What are their hours? What are their chances of being promoted? Gather all the pros and cons you can find. Find out what they love about their job . . . but also what's hard about it and what frustrates them.

Finding Agreement

The most important part of the clarify/verify/explore process is coming to the point where both your heart and your head say yes without reservation. For a job to make logical sense—"It will pay well" or "This industry is practically layoff-proof"— is good, but it's not enough. Your head can't have the only say in the matter, and neither can your heart. They both must be in full agreement. Then you can make a plan for execution to help you move forward.

At the end of the day, it comes down to the heart test. I'm about to challenge you the same way I do the callers to my show. Let's say you have three possible opportunities for work. Close your eyes and tell me, "If you could choose only one of them—*A*, *B*, or *C*—which one would it be? If you were guaranteed to be successful in all three, but had to pick just one, what does your heart want?" Almost every time, it's *A*. That's the one that's been begging both your heart and your mind, "Pick me!" That's the one.

With that choice, your head and heart ring out a *ding, ding, ding* instead of the droning game-show buzz that comes with a "no" and a big red *X*. The truth is, you were never actually unclear about which job you wanted most. You were just *afraid of picking the wrong one*. Too many people end up doing nothing because of the paralysis of analysis. You're trying to answer all the questions and look at things from every angle, which is good, but you end up doing nothing.

The easiest thing to do is just go with your gut. If you look at a type of work and think *Ooooh, yeah!*, that's a good thing because the result (your mission) outweighs any negatives you might perceive. But, if you look at it and think *Ewwww, no!*— it's probably because the result doesn't outweigh the negatives. You need to listen to both reactions, because they each can lead toward clarity. It all goes back to your wiring and the fact that you're wired differently from other people.

This process works every time. Not just for getting clear on which dream job to pursue, but for clarifying virtually any aspect of your career. The simple but powerful process of "clarify and verify" is what allows you to avoid analysis paralysis and keep moving forward.

CONCLUSION

It's Up to You

"If we do not develop our own self-awareness and become responsible for first creations, we empower other people and circumstances to shape our lives by default."

Stephen Covey

Congratulations! You've reached the end of the book, and you have your *Get Clear Career Assessment* results! Do you remember what I told you at the beginning of this book about what you would get from this? *You'll walk away knowing who you are, what you want to do, why you want to do it, where you can do it, and how you can get there.* That was a big promise, but I'm confident that's what you're taking with you.

Self-awareness is *the* advantage for personal and professional success. You have it now. You know what you do best. You know what you enjoy doing. You know the results that motivate you to get up, show up, and keep moving up.

YOU were created to fill a unique role through your work.

YOU are needed.

YOU matter deeply.

YOU have what it takes to make a difference in this world.

YOU must do it.

But this book and assessment is not all about you. It's about other people. It's about the people who need you to show up and be the best version of you—for them. You get to decide who they are, where they are, and how you will serve them.

Fear, doubt, and critics will always be present on your journey. When they appear, remind yourself of these words from President Teddy Roosevelt in his April 1910 speech at the Sorbonne in Paris:

> It is not the critic who counts; not the man who
> points out how the strong man stumbles, or where
> the doer of deeds could have done them better. The

credit belongs to the man who is actually in the arena, whose face is marred by dust and sweat and blood; who strives valiantly; who errs, who comes short again and again, because there is no effort without error and shortcoming; but who does actually strive to do the deeds; who knows the great enthusiasms, the great devotions; who spends himself in a worthy cause; who at the best knows in the end the triumph of high achievement, and who at the worst, if he fails, at least fails while daring greatly, so that his place shall never be with those cold and timid souls who neither know victory nor defeat.[8]

I want you to feel the significance of being you and doing what you were born to do. To look back on your life with the knowledge that you did your best to give your best. So be willing to fail greatly in pursuit of doing the work you're best at, work that you love, and work that impacts the world.

What does that look like for you? I can't answer that for you. The assessment can't answer that for you. As a matter of fact, there's not an assessment out there that will tell you

---

8. Theodore Roosevelt, "It Is Not the Critic Who Counts," Theodore Roosevelt Conservation Partnership, posted January 18, 2011, https://www.trcp.org/2011/01/18/it-is-not-the-critic-who-counts/.

exactly what you need to be doing. But now you're pointed in the right direction. Now it's up to you. The ball's in your court. Knowing what you know now, how are you going to get to where you want to be?

History rewards people who step out and step up. Your turn. I'm cheering you on!

TALENTS GLOSSARY

COMMUNICATION

Words are easy for you!

Talent Summary

You're gifted at sharing thoughts, feelings, and information through speaking or writing. You're known for your ability to tell a compelling story as well as your ability to express ideas clearly. You're good at understanding people, identifying messages others are trying to convey, being understood, connecting with others, and getting your point across. Articulating your thoughts and sharing them with those around you comes very naturally for you. **Areas of Work: People and Ideas**

How You Wow Others

Conversation
Listening
Speaking
Storytelling
Writing

What Others Say About You

You have a way with words.
That was written so well.
You're a great storyteller.
You explained that so clearly.
I enjoy our conversations.

Talent Traps to Avoid

Trying to solve or heal with words
Frustration when others don't communicate well

COMPASSION

Sometimes, your heart is bigger than your brain!

Talent Summary

You're always looking out for others and helping people in need. People are drawn to you—especially those with emotional, physical, or spiritual needs. You pay attention to people who are hurting or marginalized, validate them, give them a voice, and take action on their behalf. You're skilled at finding ways to make people's lives better, whether it's through education, health care, public service, or ministry. You're able to see the world through the eyes of others. **Areas of Work: People and Ideas**

How You Wow Others

Understanding situations
Protecting others
Listening
Building relationships
Serving those in need

What Others Say About You

You put others before yourself.
You have a servant's heart.
You're so generous.
Thank you for keeping us safe.
You helped me see that need.

Talent Traps to Avoid

Burning yourself out by overserving (becomes your identity)
Giving help when it's counterproductive

CONNECTION

You've never met a stranger!

Talent Summary

You're skilled at getting to know people and you form relationships with ease. You have no problem sparking conversation and turning strangers into friends. You remember details about others—like what kind of puppy they got for Christmas or how many kids they have. You have a wide network of social and professional relationships, including some influential or powerful people. It's easy for you to connect the people in your circles with one another. **Area of Work: People**

How You Wow Others

Meeting people
Finding common interests
Introducing people
Building relationships
Staying in touch

What Others Say About You

It seems like you know everybody.
You're such a people person.
Can you introduce me to _____?
We have a lot in common.
It feels like I've known you a long time.

Talent Traps to Avoid

Becoming a relationship vampire (using people)
Spreading yourself too thin with too many relationships

DISCERNMENT

You could replace Judge Judy!

Talent Summary

You're perceptive about people and situations and have a knack for "telling it like it is." While others might struggle to understand their thoughts, emotions, and experiences, you help draw them out and lead them into self-awareness. You're quick to recognize patterns of behavior and you're interested in understanding why people do what they do. You're known for making wise decisions and being comfortable making judgment calls about people or circumstances. **Areas of Work: People and Ideas**

How You Wow Others

Simplifying complex situations
Predicting outcomes
Seeing the big picture
Digging deeper to get insight
Reading people

What Others Say About You

You read people so well.
You're a great judge of character.
I need your wisdom.
I appreciate your perspective.
What do you predict?

Talent Traps to Avoid

Being overly critical of others
Overanalyzing what others are saying/doing

EXECUTION

You get more done before breakfast than most people do all day!

Talent Summary

You're highly productive and good at checking things off your to-do list. You pay attention to the work that's assigned to you and take your responsibilities seriously. You're good at setting goals, keeping track of progress, and taking initiative to improve your work. Always ready to take the first step, you're action-oriented, practical, and focused. You look at the end result of a project or task and think about what steps you need to take to get it done on schedule. **Areas of Work: Processes and Objects**

How You Wow Others

Keeping track of details
Staying focused
Completing a list
Setting and achieving goals
Taking action

What Others Say About You

You stay on top of things.
I need you to make this happen.
You're so productive.
Can you help us get this done?
Thanks for keeping us on track.

Talent Traps to Avoid

Trying to do everything yourself (being self-consumed)
Focusing on completing lists instead of true priorities

IMAGINATION

You get ideas in the middle of your ideas!

Talent Summary

You're skilled at coming up with new ideas, always imagining how to connect future possibilities with current realities. Expressing your creativity comes naturally to you—whether through music, painting, inventions, stories, drama, or business ideas. You're curious and playful, fascinated by ideas, and always open to the next thing. You draw connections between different ideas, events, and problems that others may not see. You like to absorb information. **Areas of Work: Ideas, Processes, and Objects**

How You Wow Others

Big-picture thinking
Creative problem-solving
Starting new things
Vision-casting
Seeing things others don't

What Others Say About You

You're so creative!
You have great ideas.
Wow! That is so interesting.
I've never thought of it that way.
You're so inspiring!

Talent Traps to Avoid

Great ideas getting lost in a sea of good ideas
Chasing an unrealistic idea

INSPECTION

You walk into a room and notice everything that should be improved!

Talent Summary

You're highly observant and you catch the details that other people miss. You have an ability to accurately critique the world around you. You process things efficiently while seeing a variety of perspectives and weighing all the possibilities effectively. You're good at researching, understanding how things work, and engaging in intellectual activities or discussions. You're constantly gathering new information about events, systems, objects, people, and ideas. **Areas of Work: Ideas and Processes**

How You Wow Others

Curiosity
Attention to details
Researching information
Critical thinking
Observations

What Others Say About You

You're a good problem-solver.
Will you review this for accuracy?
You seem to know a lot of random facts.
Will you research some options?
I'm so glad you caught that issue.

Talent Traps to Avoid

Being distracted by something new to learn or observe
Being too critical or negative of people and projects

INSTRUCTION

You're a trusted guide!

Talent Summary

You're gifted at passing along information, sharing knowledge about a subject, and teaching skills to others. You work well with other people and have the ability to help them increase in what they know and what they can do. You're good at developing systematic methods for learning and instruction, like lesson plans, workout routines, presentations, and curriculum. You find it easy to take complex ideas or systems and create ways for others to understand them. **Areas of Work: People, Ideas, and Processes**

How You Wow Others

Gathering information
Developing learning plans
Coaching others
Encouraging
Simplifying learning

What Others Say About You

You're a great teacher.
Your training is so effective.
I love how you coach others.
You've helped me learn so much.
That presentation was super clear!

Talent Traps to Avoid

Getting frustrated when others don't get your teaching
Being closed-minded to new ways of learning and instruction

JUSTICE

You stand for what's right!

Talent Summary

You have a strong sense of right and wrong and you're quick to defend the vulnerable. You have a high "justice meter" and you can imagine yourself in others' situations. You're skilled at dealing with matters of morality, lawfulness, and fairness. You're good at protecting the weak and challenging injustice. You have above-average confrontation skills. You stand up against people who are abusing their power or getting away with breaking the rules. **Areas of Work: People and Ideas**

How You Wow Others

Critical thinking
Defining right and wrong
Putting others first
Seeking social change
Standing up for your beliefs

What Others Say About You

You care so much about people.
Thank you for taking a stand.
I appreciate how you speak up.
You're making a difference.
I admire your courage.

Talent Traps to Avoid

Pressuring others to align with your morality or beliefs
Always putting a cause or the needs of others before yourself

LOGIC

You eat problems for breakfast!

Talent Summary

You're skilled at critical thinking and using reason to solve problems. You're able to keep a level head as you assess multiple points of view and analyze complex issues. You're good at connecting dots, articulating arguments, and strategic planning. You understand there are systems and principles that govern certain aspects of life—and you work to understand those patterns and rules. You dig into details and do research before coming to a conclusion. **Areas of Work: Ideas and Processes**

How You Wow Others

Analysis
Decision-making
Planning
Strategy
Problem-solving

What Others Say About You

You're a great thinker.
I need your opinion.
Help me solve this problem.
Your explanation made this super clear.
Help me make sense of this.

Talent Traps to Avoid

Overplanning and not executing—paralysis by analysis
Frequently correcting others and coming across as a know-it-all

ORGANIZATION

You bring order to the world around you!

Talent Summary

You're good at creating order out of chaos and inventing or improving systems. Coming up with new and better processes is easy and you enjoy managing all the variables in a complex situation. You're able to grasp the big picture of a project, task, or idea and then work backward to see how all the parts come together. You operate well with rules, routine, and clear expectations. Spending a Saturday organizing a messy closet would be a piece of cake for you. **Areas of Work: Ideas and Processes**

How You Wow Others

Planning
Noticing and organizing details
List-making
Implementing systems
Coming up with solutions

What Others Say About You

You keep us on track.
You're so organized.
This place would fall apart without you.
How do you keep up with everything?
I knew you would find the information.

Talent Traps to Avoid

Not allowing space for spontaneity
Judging those who aren't as organized

PERSUASION

You can move people to think, feel, and act!

Talent Summary

You're skilled at influencing people to change their beliefs or take a specific action. You use your ability to speak or write to inspire others, appeal to their reason, encourage them to do things differently, make them aware of an important issue, or convince them of some truth. You have a knack for promoting products and ideas and getting people to buy in. You have a dynamic and compelling personality. You enjoy meeting and working with new people. **Areas of Work: People and Ideas**

How You Wow Others

Leading people
Selling
Advising
Marketing
Coaching others

What Others Say About You

You're so persuasive.
You could sell anything.
You're very influential.
I had never thought of trying it that way.
I would follow you anywhere.

Talent Traps to Avoid

Not knowing when to turn it off (always promoting)
Pushing people too hard too soon (people aren't projects)

PASSIONS GLOSSARY

ADVISING

You love sharing your opinion!

Passion Summary

You come alive when you're offering guidance, suggestions, and advice to other people. You're naturally inclined to help others solve their problems—whether it's in their personal or professional lives. You enjoy combining your discernment with your critical-thinking skills to help people create a clear path that allows them to move forward. You're energized by brainstorming ideas, creating strategies, and helping people set and meet their goals. **Areas of Work: People and Ideas**

Work You Love to Do

Talking through a problem
Consulting with a client
Listening and asking questions
Understanding points of view
Demonstrating empathy
Digging into alternate solutions
Simplifying a problem
Offering encouragement to others
Providing instruction and direction
Helping others set goals

Passion Pitfalls to Avoid

Always insisting that it's your way or the highway
Offering unwanted advice

ADVOCATING

You love to fight for what's right!

Passion Summary

You have a deep desire to use your voice to speak on behalf of a certain cause or group of people. You've got a crusader mentality. You're persuasive, articulate, and passionate about defending the rights of the vulnerable or raising awareness about an important issue. You want to protect the weak and challenge injustice. You long to be part of a movement that creates meaningful change—whether that be for one person, a community, or even society in general. **Areas of Work: People and Ideas**

Work You Love to Do

Starting and leading a cause
Being an agent of change
Fighting for the rights of others
Protecting others from harm
Exposing the "bad guys"
Educating others to help them
Communicating a solution
Seeking social justice
Organizing thoughts and people
Persuasive speaking and writing

Passion Pitfalls to Avoid

Taking on too much and trying to fight too many battles
Mental and emotional burnout

ANALYZING

You love to look at everything from multiple angles!

Passion Summary

You lose track of time when you're examining an issue or an object and breaking it down into its various parts so you can better understand its whole. You're fascinated by patterns and connections. You enjoy digging deep so you can understand the root cause of the topic, problem, or task at hand. You're inclined to reject wishful thinking and emotional decision-making so you can focus on the facts, understand key factors, and come to a sound conclusion. **Areas of Work: Processes and Objects**

Work You Love to Do

Solving problems
Observing and understanding details
Figuring out how things work
Looking for patterns and key factors
Improving processes and productivity
Examining all the details of a project
Critical thinking related to a problem or task
Researching an issue
Exploring various options
Simplifying complex ideas or problems

Passion Pitfalls to Avoid

Becoming disconnected from others
Paralysis by analysis leads you to not do anything

CAREGIVING

You love to take care of others!

Passion Summary

You're energized when you spend your time helping others. You love providing care—short-term or even for an extended period of time—to people with physical, emotional, or mental challenges. You feel drawn to helping children and adults who can't care for themselves, and you spend your energy to serve them. You're naturally generous, compassionate, empathetic, and patient with people in need. Serving and sacrificing for others gives you the juice. **Area of Work: People**

Work You Love to Do

Listening to the needs of others
Guiding others in conversation
Talking through personal issues
Teaching others to care for themselves
Offering rehabilitative care
Providing emotional and physical support
Encouraging those in distress
Nurturing children
Advocating for the needs of others
Serving people in need

Passion Pitfalls to Avoid

Forgetting to take care of yourself
Overcommitment to the needs of others

CREATING

You love imagining and doing all things new!

Passion Summary

You love creating new things or being an entrepreneur. You thrive when you're creating aesthetic and beautiful things or starting a new business. You enjoy writing, painting, sculpting, dancing, or other creative activity. You lose track of time when you're brainstorming all the creative ways you can bring a plan, concept, project, or business to life. You enjoy writing or designing things that add innovation or beauty to the world. You enjoy seeing your ideas come to life. **Areas of Work: Ideas and Objects**

Work You Love to Do

Designing logos, graphics, or animations
Writing a screenplay or theater show
Starting a new business
Designing shoes or apparel
Creating written or spoken content
Inventing new products
Painting or sculpting works of art
Writing music, songs, and soundtracks
Brainstorming new ideas with others
Landscaping a yard or business

Passion Pitfalls to Avoid

Not seeing a project to its completion
Always looking for a new thing to create

FINISHING

You love checking things off a list!

Passion Summary

You experience tremendous satisfaction when you or your team bring a project or task over the finish line. You love accuracy and attention to detail. You always make sure that all the boxes are checked before you give your stamp of approval on a project or task. You're disciplined and careful in the work you do. You take a lot of pride in practicing excellence in the ordinary and following through with the tasks that have been assigned to you or your team. **Areas of Work: Processes and Objects**

Work You Love to Do

Creating a list of tasks that need to be done
Checking items off a list
Being organized
Organizing the details of a project
Analyzing why a task is behind schedule
Creating systems for organization
Leading others to execute a plan
Project management
Keeping a team on a schedule
Collaborating on a project

Passion Pitfalls to Avoid

Viewing people as pawns to complete a project
Becoming too aggressive in setting timelines

LEADING

You love to guide people!

Passion Summary

You come alive when you're using your skills in communication to influence other people. It gives you the juice to impact the actions, opinions, and beliefs of others. You thrive when you're with people discussing meaningful ideas or spearheading a movement that's important to you. You feel excited at the opportunity to share your voice, opinion, ideas, or solutions with people. You're comfortable standing before others to share your thoughts and opinions. **Areas of Work: People and Ideas**

Work You Love to Do

Inspiring others to action
Leading a team
Helping people reach their potential
Communicating to an audience
Motivating others toward a goal
Changing thoughts and actions
Sharing ideas that matter
Encouraging change and growth
Challenging the status quo
Writing a book to guide others

Passion Pitfalls to Avoid

Seeing everyone as a project you can improve
Becoming closed-minded to other voices

MAKING

You love to use your brain and hands to fix it or build it!

Passion Summary

You love making things with your hands. The physical experience of making original or useful things gives you the juice. You feel most productive when you're making things either by inventing, building, or constructing them. You thrive when you're using your skills to make tangible things that people will use to make their lives more comfortable, more enjoyable, or more efficient. You enjoy using a variety of tools. You find great pleasure in putting all the pieces together. **Areas of Work: Ideas and Objects**

Work You Love to Do

Building with your hands
Mechanic
Home construction
Making new gadgets and tools
Auto assembly
Manufacturing
Furniture building and carpentry
Computer assembly
Engineering
Using new tools and equipment

Passion Pitfalls to Avoid

Being too focused on perfectionism that you never finish
Being so project-focused you miss personal connections

PERFORMING

You love to come through under pressure!

Passion Summary

You come alive when you're doing what you're good at in front of an audience—performing! You enjoy the feeling of pressure that comes from having all eyes on you. You thrive in the spotlight, draw energy from the crowd, and you're eager for opportunities to get in front of people—whether that's performing music, acting, or speaking about a favorite topic on a stage, on the radio, or in film. Competition is fun for you, and you're energized by challenges and rewards. **Areas of Work: People and Ideas**

Work You Love to Do

Speaking to a group
Broadcasting
Acting
Singing solo or in a group
Being in front of an audience
Performing under pressure
Preparation
Connecting with an audience
Writing scripts
The performing arts

Passion Pitfalls to Avoid

Letting your performance determine your value
Forgetting to rest long enough to recharge

PLANNING

You love to connect details, action items, and goals!

Passion Summary

You lose track of time when you're coming up with a plan for a specific project or important endeavor. You enjoy tracking down all the relevant details, thinking through your options, and deciding on a course of action. You love to strategize about how you'll overcome potential obstacles. You raise your hand to help plan your family vacation and don't think twice about putting all the details in a beautiful spreadsheet so everyone can get on the same page. **Area of Work: Ideas and Processes**

Work You Love to Do

Creating strategies
Thinking about the future
Logistical details
Organizing information
Procedures and processes
Analyzing data
Coordinating details
Testing ideas
Analyzing information
Researching details

Passion Pitfalls to Avoid

Becoming a control freak
Being paralyzed by the unknown

PROMOTING

You love being the cheerleader!

Passion Summary

You thrive on promoting products or ideas to people who need to hear about them. You get energized by explaining all of the features, details, benefits, and advantages of what you have to offer. Because you believe so strongly in the product or idea, you want to tell everyone about it. You find it easy to persuade others with your words. You're drawn to sales, advertising, or publicity as a means to express how important your idea, product, or service is to others. **Areas of Work: People and Ideas**

Work You Love to Do

Marketing products
Selling ideas and items
Creating an advertising plan
Storytelling
Public relations
Social media promotion
Vision-casting
Training a team
Networking with others
Writing promotional copy

Passion Pitfalls to Avoid

Overselling and losing credibility
Promoting something or someone you don't believe in

PROTECTING

You love making people feel safe!

Passion Summary

You're passionate about defending the vulnerable and shielding people from danger. Your deep desire is to make sure the people, things, or causes you care about are safe and protected. You're highly aware of potential threats and work hard to diminish those threats. You come alive when you're standing up to the "bad guys." You're skilled at using phone calls, conversations, physical strength, situational awareness, and written communication to protect others. **Area of Work: People**

Work You Love to Do

Advocating for others
Sharing information
Defending those in need
Serving others
Providing caregiving
Prosecuting the bad guys
Confronting issues
Training others
Mentoring
Monitoring security

Passion Pitfalls to Avoid

Protecting others but not those closest to you
Becoming overwhelmed by the number of people who need help

RESEARCHING

You love digging in to learn new things!

Passion Summary

Digging in and gathering information gives you the juice. You're excited by discovery, curiosity, problem-solving, and learning new things. You lose track of time when you're reading books or watching media about a topic that interests you. You want to understand the true origin of a source and you take pride in sticking to the facts, revising theories, and investigating a matter fully. When you're working on a project, others recognize your ability to research the details. **Areas of Work: Ideas and Processes**

Work You Love to Do

Researching information
Investigation
Testing ideas and options
Experimenting with alternatives
Learning about a topic
Predicting outcomes
Providing new information
Presenting details
Strategic thinking
Interviewing

Passion Pitfalls to Avoid

Becoming obsessed with the search for new information
Gathering so many options and opinions that you get lost

SOLVING

You love making things work!

Passion Summary

You lose track of time when you're fixing something—whether it's a mechanical, technical, systematic, or mathematical problem—because you enjoy it so much. You love searching for answers and explanations. You're great at solving mysteries and clearing up confusion. You thrive on making broken things better and providing a solution to a puzzle. Where there's a problem to solve, others count on you to dig in and find a solution. You're known as a problem-solver. **Areas of Work: People, Processes, and Objects**

Work You Love to Do

Problem-solving
Fixing broken things
Improving processes
Inventing something new
Testing ideas
Researching options
Building new things
Analyzing results
Developing innovations
Restoring something

Passion Pitfalls to Avoid

Trying to solve so many problems that it slows you down
Not knowing when to let a problem go

TEACHING

You love showing people the way!

Passion Summary

You come alive when you're sharing knowledge, opening up people's minds to new ideas, and helping them learn new skills. You lose track of time when you're thinking of new ways to communicate what you know to others and inspire them to change. You enjoy teaching about something and seeing people move from point A to point B as they improve. You appreciate the mastery of a subject and recognize the important difference it can make in the lives of others. **Areas of Work: People, Ideas, and Processes**

Work You Love to Do

Coaching others
Leading training sessions
Communicating to a team
Providing feedback
Assessing a problem
Motivating others
Guiding a process
Learning new information
Connecting with others
Mentoring

Passion Pitfalls to Avoid

Judging yourself by students' performance
Not continuously learning and adapting

MISSION GLOSSARY

ACHIEVEMENT

You want to produce wins.

Mission Summary

You feel significance when you achieve a goal, exceed an expectation, and beat the competition. Winning energizes you. Challenges motivate and inspire you to take action—because you're always looking for the next opportunity to win. You strive to have the best idea in a meeting, make record sales, or lead the highest-performing team. You get excited when others notice and applaud your results. You want and need scoreboards to track your progress.

Results That Fire You Up

Exceeding your goal
Getting promoted
Being the top performer
Pulling off the unexpected
Turning a company, team, or results around

Mission Missteps

Chasing a challenge that distracts you from your purpose
Becoming "me" focused instead of "we" focused

CREATION

You want to produce something new or better.

Mission Summary

You're motivated by creating original, better, and different products or services. You feel significance when you're creating new things for others. Whether it be an idea, a piece of art, a business, a book, a song, a makeover, a design, or clothing, you want to imagine a new thing that makes an impact on others and brings value to their lives. You're motivated and energized by originality, beauty, and venturing into new territory where no one else has been.

Results That Fire You Up

Developing a new product
Coming up with new content
Building something new
Writing a story, poem, or song
Designing a room, website, or clothing

Mission Missteps

Too much dreaming and not enough doing
Not being open to collaboration

EFFICIENCY

You want to produce order and excellence.

Mission Summary

You feel significance when you're creating and maintaining efficient systems and results. Order gives you energy while disorder drains you. You look for order and efficiency as a sign of quality. When observing disorder and dysfunction in systems or policies, you instinctively see or wonder about the source of the problem and the solution. You look for ways to establish new and better procedures that will result in a better overall system or an end product.

Results That Fire You Up

A completed checklist or finished project
Finishing a task or project before a deadline
Creating a more efficient workflow system
Improving a slow process
Organizing files, communication, or a room

Mission Missteps

Pursuing efficiency at the expense of others
Having an "I can do it better" attitude that makes you take on too much

INFLUENCE

You want to produce change in people.

Mission Summary

You believe people can change—and you want to be a part of their change. It's meaningful for you to connect with people, confront their challenges, and convince them that they don't have to stay where they are. Using your influence to produce change energizes you and gives you a sense of significance. You're driven to cast a vision for all that could be. You want to lead people and causes. Activating and guiding people and teams to their desired future is not pressure, it's preferred.

Results That Fire You Up

Counseling a person to transformation
Selling a product or service
Leading a team to wins
Training an individual or a team
Communicating content

Mission Missteps

Prioritizing building your platform over investing in people
Focusing on those you *didn't* influence instead of those you did

SERVICE

You want to produce assistance for people.

Mission Summary

Helping others fills your heart, gives you energy, and creates a feeling of significance. You desire to lift people, protect people, and care for people in whatever ways you can. Your eyes and ears are always scanning for the person who is in need—and you're motivated to bring them relief in some form. While others are reluctant to jump in and help, you're ready to help at a moment's notice. You're driven by a desire to heal, to include, to listen, and to love others.

Results That Fire You Up

Bringing aid to those in need
Comforting people in a time of crisis
Satisfying an unhappy customer
Protecting the vulnerable
Helping someone else succeed

Mission Missteps

Serving others so much that you burn out
Finding your identity in how you help others

SOLUTION

You want to produce fixes for problems.

Mission Summary

Problems don't scare you—they energize you. When things don't work, you get to work because you're a problem-solver. The more problems you solve, the better your day is—and that makes you feel significant to your organization. You believe you can always find a solution to any problem and you're quick to dive into analysis and troubleshooting to figure it out. In fact, you find meaning in identifying problems and then pushing past them.

Results That Fire You Up

Figuring out complex problems
Resolving conflict between others
Repairing something that's broken
Improving processes and procedures
Innovating something that's outdated

Mission Missteps

Creating problems to validate your value
Assuming your solution is the only way

TESTIMONIALS

The *Get Clear Career Assessment* gave me clarity, just like Ken said! I always knew in my heart my talents, passions, and mission—but through the questions I was able to see the big picture, dial it in, and broaden the opportunities on my horizon with confidence. –Joseph K.

On point and relative in business today. The results made me focus on a career that is pertinent to me and that targets my interests, skills, and helps me build industry connections. –Liza J.

It was helpful for me to see the results and visualize myself in the different positions. It confirmed some things I already believed and gave me the courage to move forward into the workforce after solely being a stay-at-home mom of six for the past 12 years. –Paris K.

My son needed confidence and clarity surrounding his class, major, and career choices midway through his undergraduate degree. The Assessment helped him know himself better and understand that we all have natural talents and passions! It gave us language to talk about his authentic self, which helped him feel known. We even used it to discuss the part-time jobs he might prefer while he works to fund his college costs in combination with his scholarship and our contribution. Thank you! –Amy S.

This assessment gave me more clarity than I expected. I have been recommending it to all my friends. WOW! What a game changer for me! –Angela L.

I took the assessment, and it helped me realize I was exactly where I was supposed to be! Thanks, Ken! –Daniel L.

I believe it is spot on and a great tool to provide focus on what I should look for next in my career. –Walter B.

Absolutely loved the assessment. It was very helpful for me to know more about my purpose. I will definitely share with others how helpful this was to me. Thank you! –David S.

The assessment nailed me completely in terms of not only my strengths but my potential weaknesses as well. I appreciate having the potential pitfalls/weaknesses called out as well so I can be fully aware of them. Thank you! –Lauren L.

Definitely provided clarity and helped me put my passion and purpose into words. Worth the purchase for sure! –Jenna C.

The top three talents and passions have given me new language about who God created me to be and how I get to bring more of His Kingdom into the world around me. –John B.

Great insights and great product! –Alan S.

The *Get Clear Career Assessment* really helped me understand how to make sense of different aspects of myself. I learned how my talents and my passions work together toward a mission I care about. This helped me as I was in the process of switching jobs. –Margareta A.

This assessment was more helpful than I imagined. It is completely accurate about me. It showed me things I had never considered as career strengths before! It got me thinking differently about what careers might work for me. The most helpful thing to me is how clear it is. –Laura C.

This assessment was very detailed and insightful. It brought light to possible reasons why I have felt discontent and discouraged in my career. There is a peace that replaced some guilt I felt. –Heather S.

It will steer you in the right direction; just be honest with yourself. –J.M.

I took the *Get Clear Career Assessment* and it blew me away. I had a feeling where my talents lay but this assessment helped to narrow down what Ken Coleman would say is my sweet spot. Because of this assessment, I am starting a new season and can't wait. –Nicole H.

This assessment really helped me get clear on where to go next in my career. It was so accurate and helped me put words to my talents and passions. I would recommend this to everyone! –Kate S.

**KEN COLEMAN** is a two-time national bestselling author and host of *The Ken Coleman Show*. His mission is to help people win at work. Whether you're looking to grow personally, advance professionally, or lead more effectively, Ken is here for you. His Get Clear Career Assessment has helped hundreds of thousands of people discover who they are and where they want to go in their career. Ken is also a regular co-host of *The Ramsey Show*, the second-largest talk show in the nation. You can follow him on YouTube, Instagram, Tik-Tok, Facebook, Twitter, and at kencoleman.com.

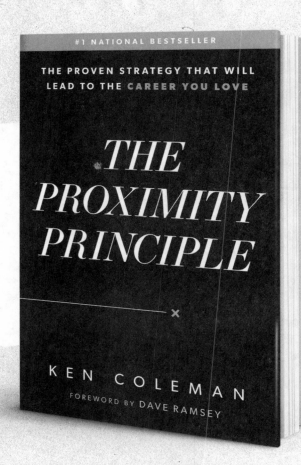

Start Pursuing a Career You Love

Now that you have clarity about the work you're wired for, it's time to start making connections in the industry you want to be a part of. Ken Coleman will guide you toward the people you need to meet and the places you need to be in order find your dream job.

kencoleman.com